The Alphabet

Aa Bb Cc Dd
Ee Ff Gg Hh Ii
Jj Kk Ll Mm
Nn Oo Pp Qq
Rr Ss Tt Uu Vv
Ww Xx Yy Zz

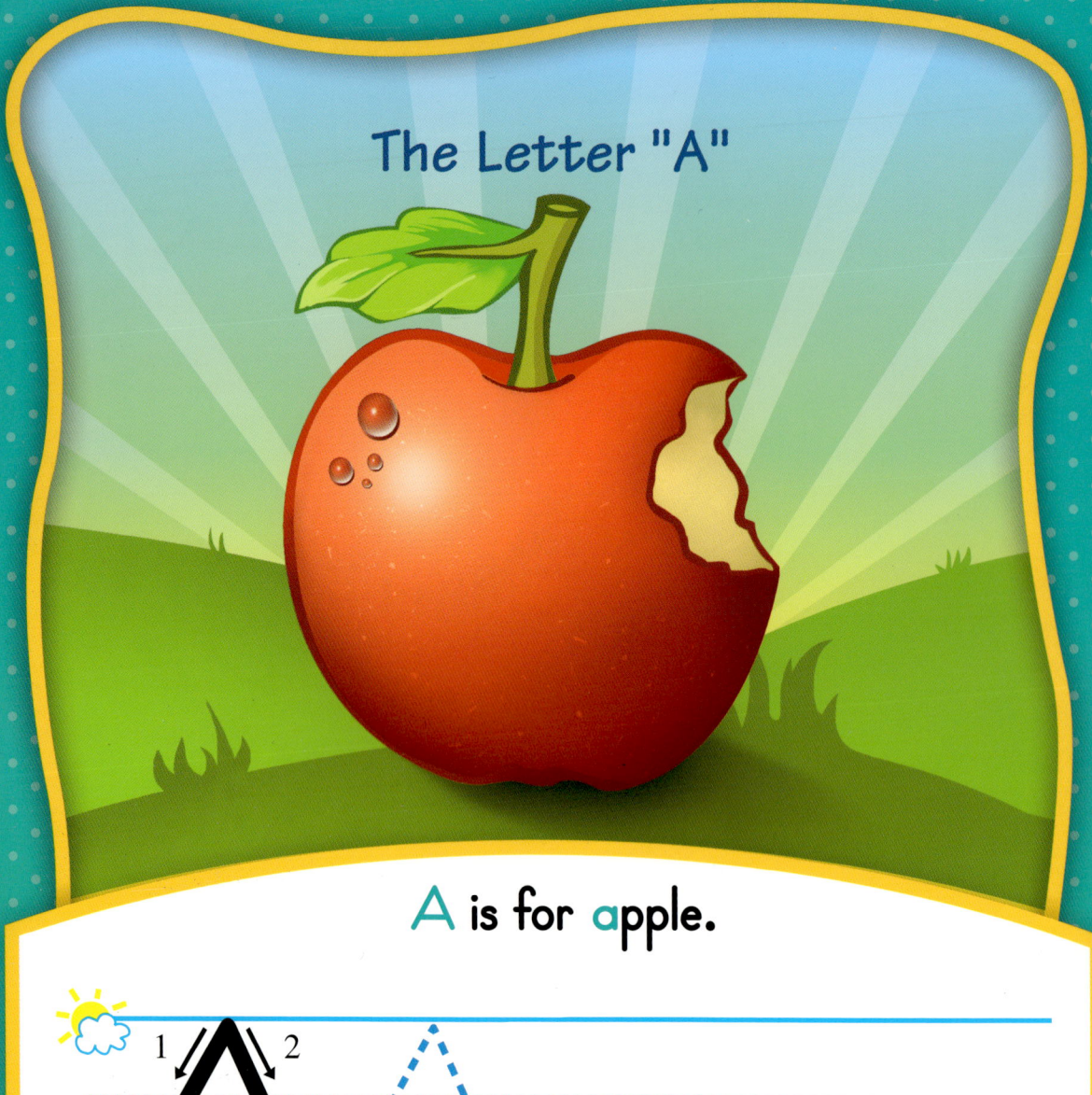

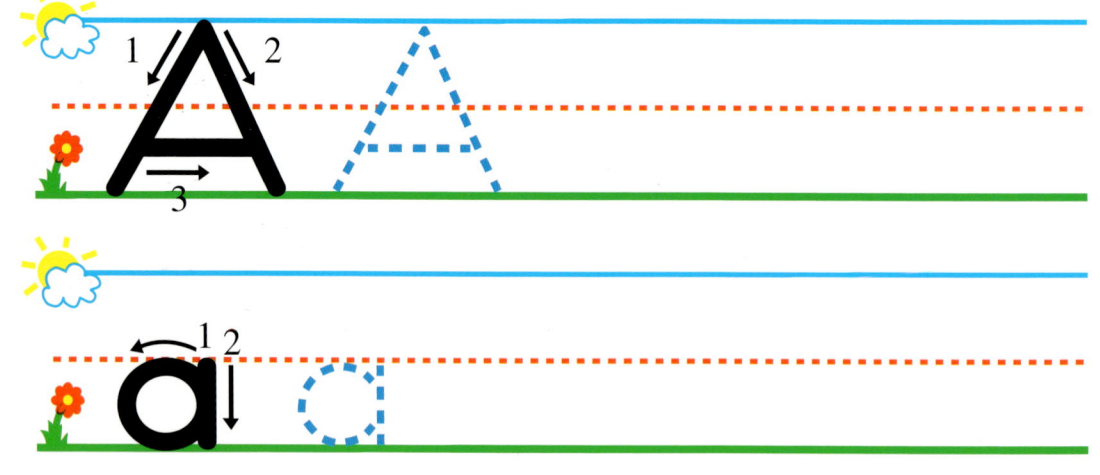

The Letter "A"

A is for apple.

The Letter "B"

B is for ball.

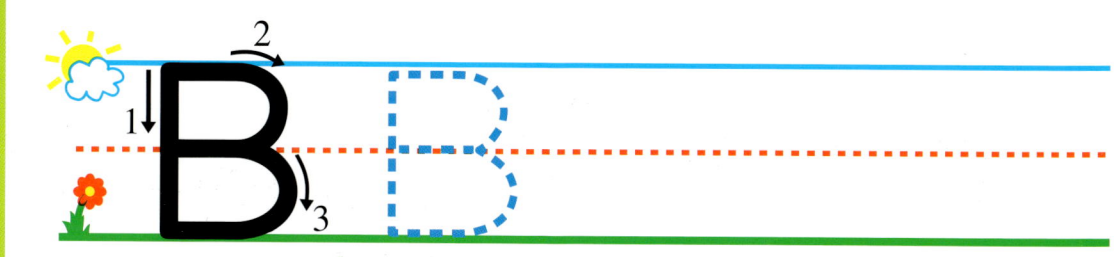

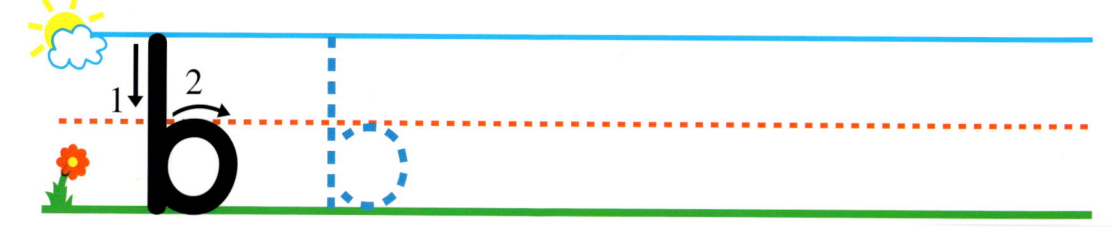

The Letter "C"

C is for corn.

The Letter "D"

D is for duck.

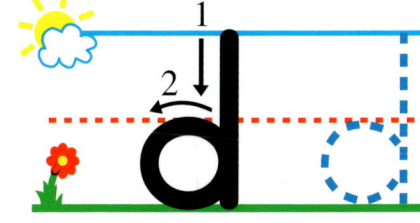

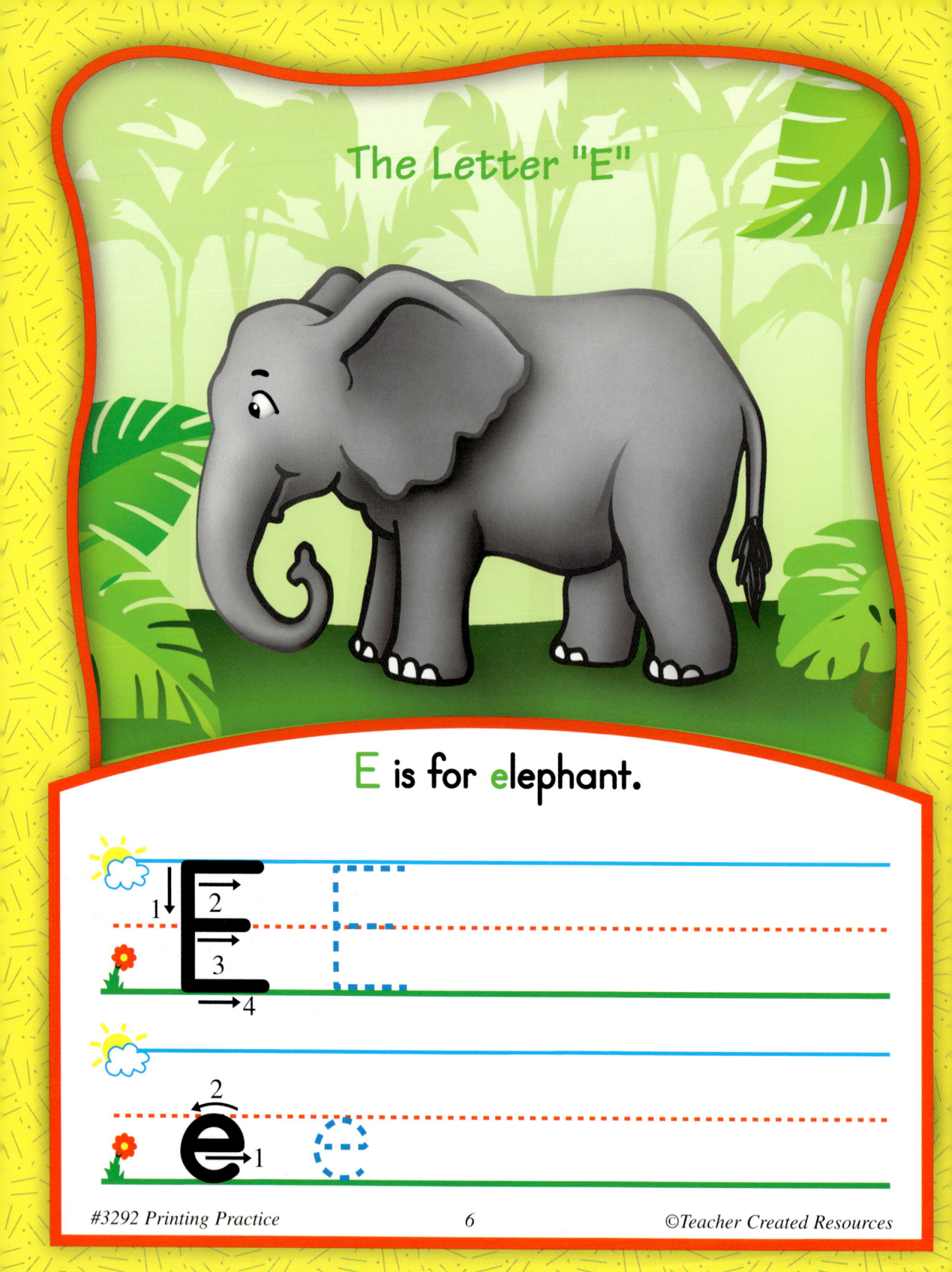

The Letter "E"

E is for **e**lephant.

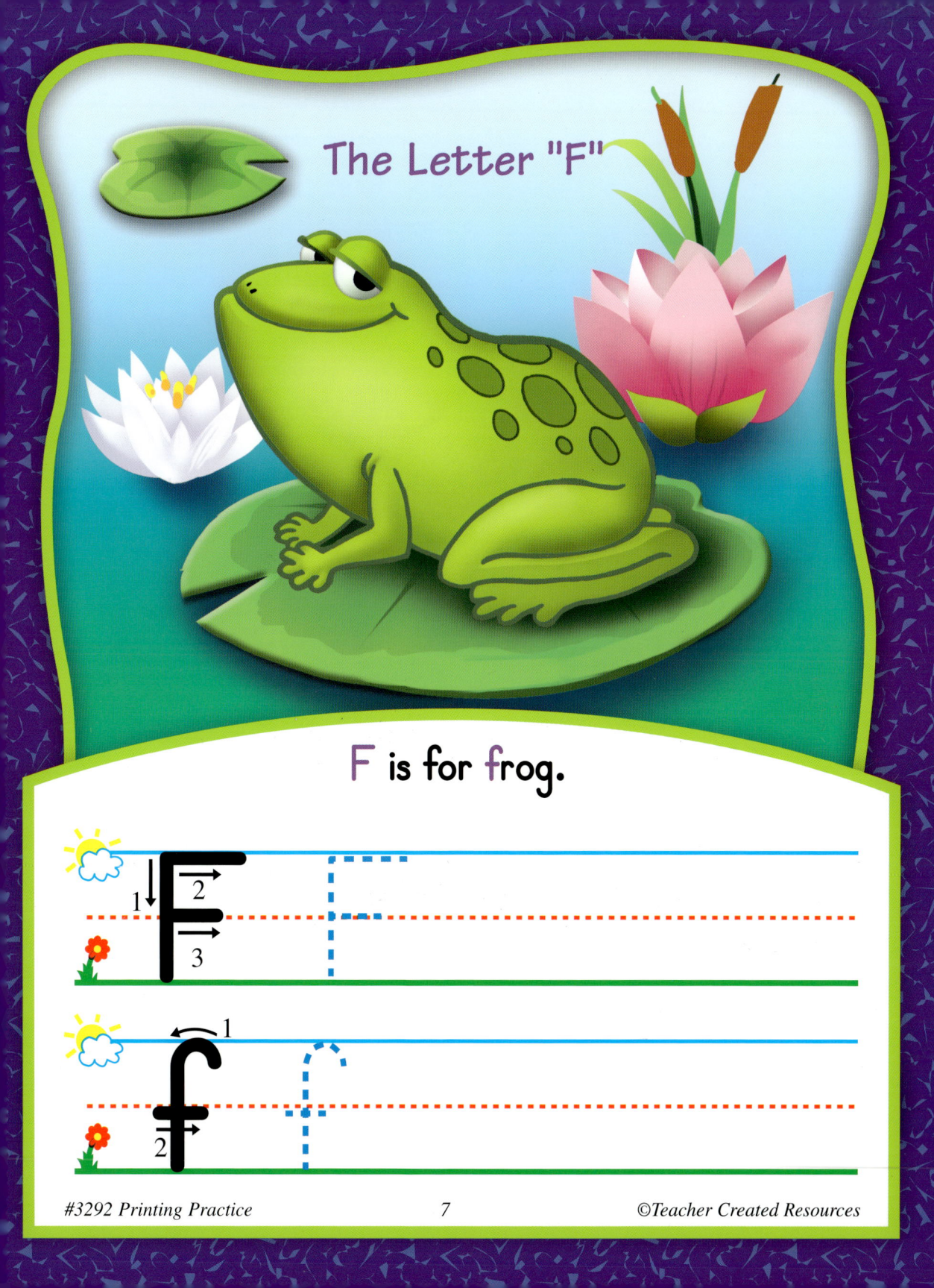

The Letter "F"

F is for frog.

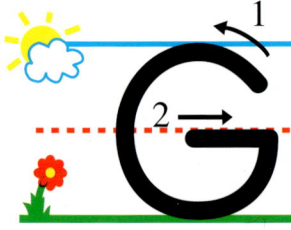

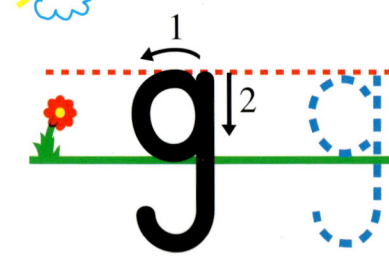

The Letter "G"

G is for goat.

The Letter "H"

H is for hat.

The Letter "I"

I is for ice cream.

The Letter "J"

J is for jam.

#3292 Printing Practice

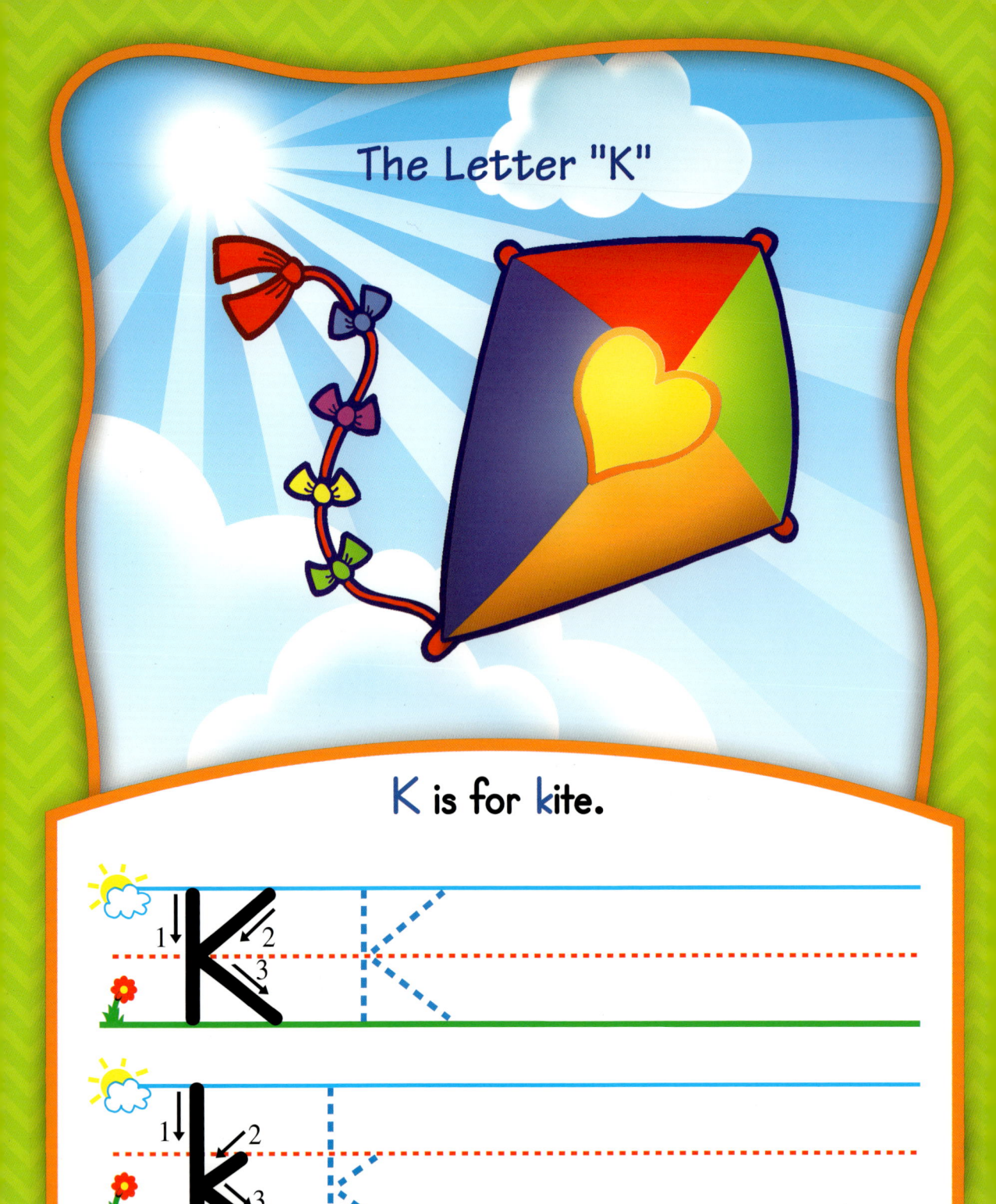

The Letter "K"

K is for kite.

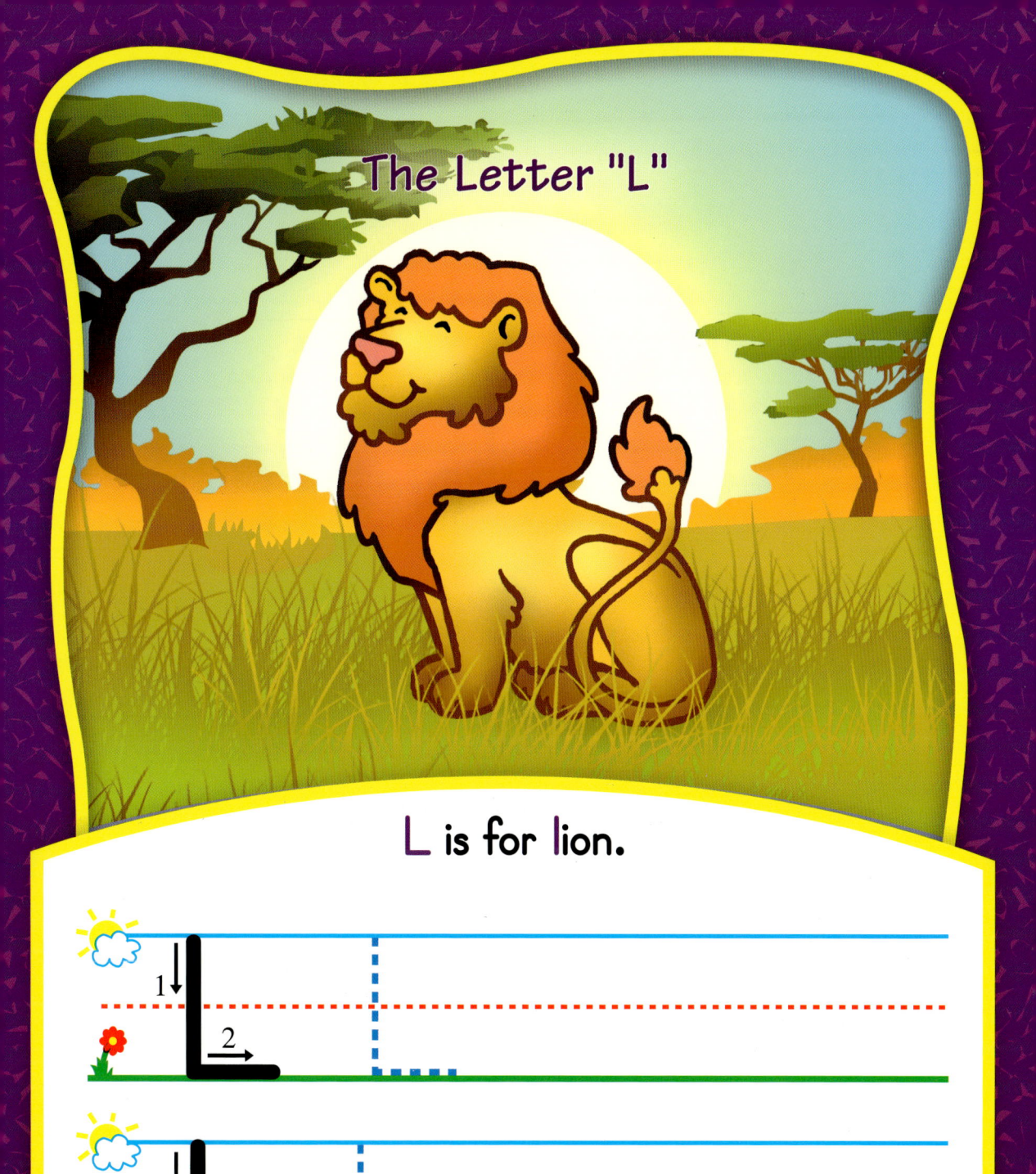

The Letter "L"

L is for lion.

The Letter "M"

M is for mouse.

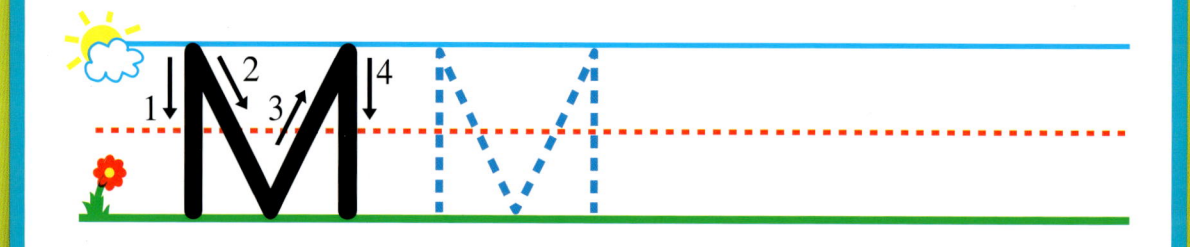

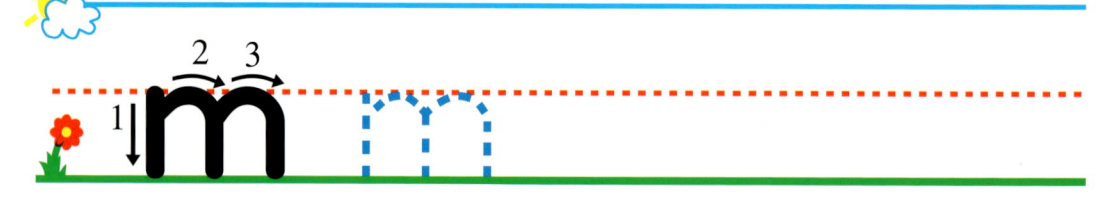

The Letter "N"

N is for **n**est.

The Letter "O"

O is for octopus.

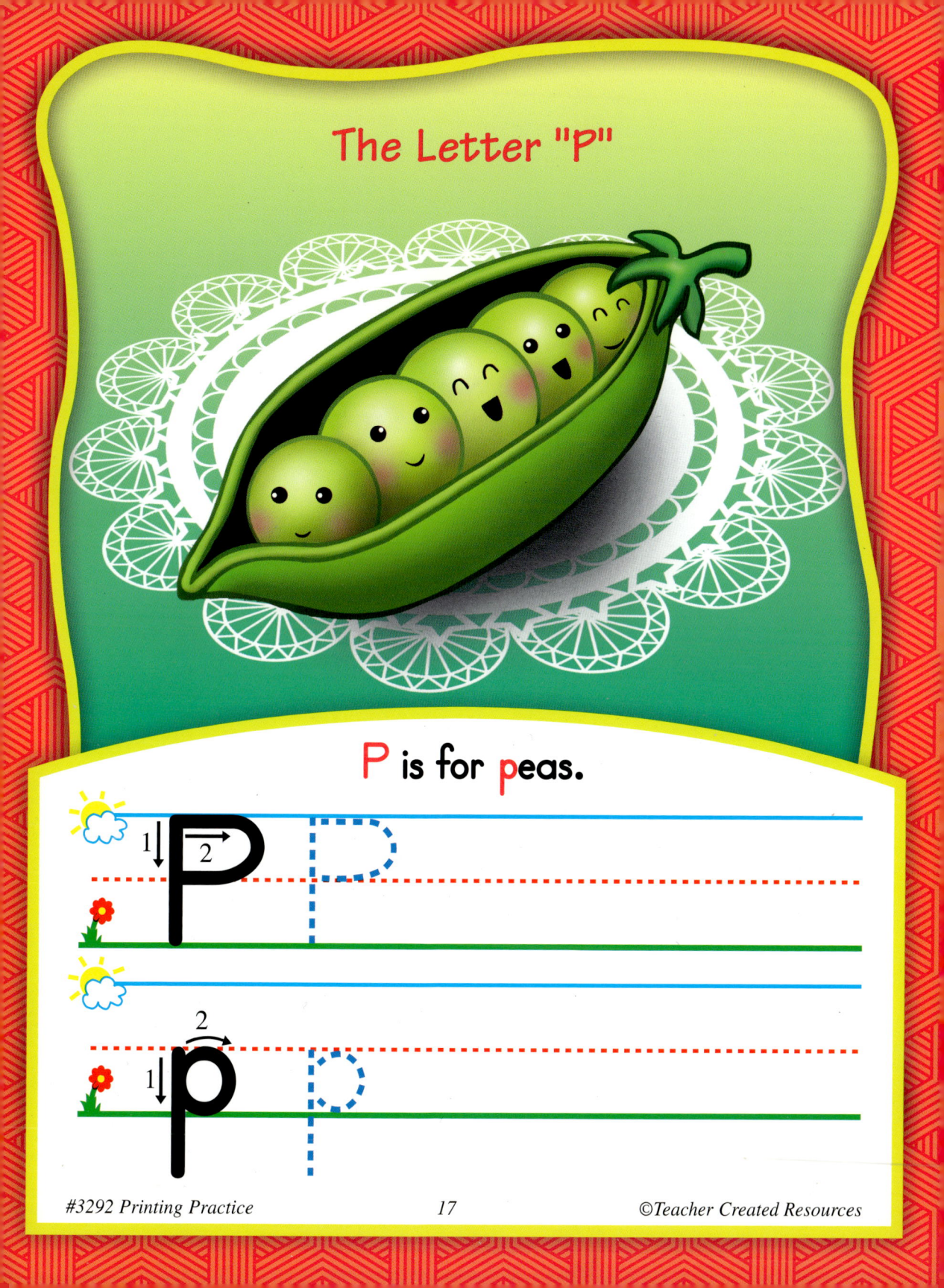

The Letter "P"

P is for peas.

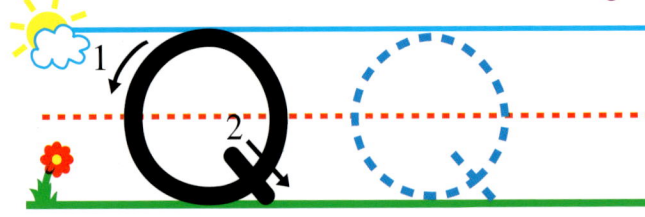

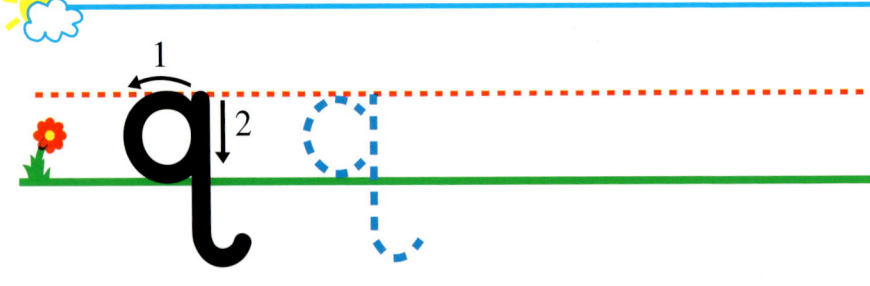

The Letter "Q"

Q is for queen.

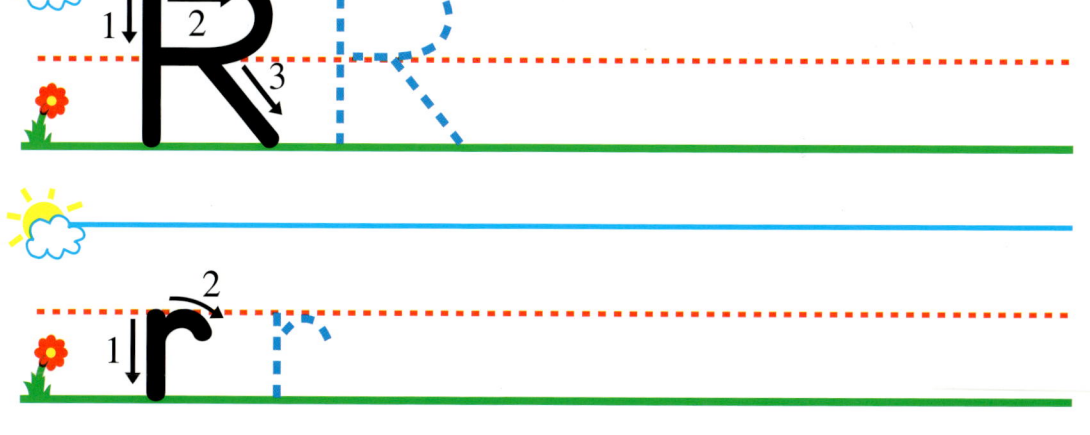

The Letter "R"

R is for rabbit.

The Letter "S"

S is for sun.

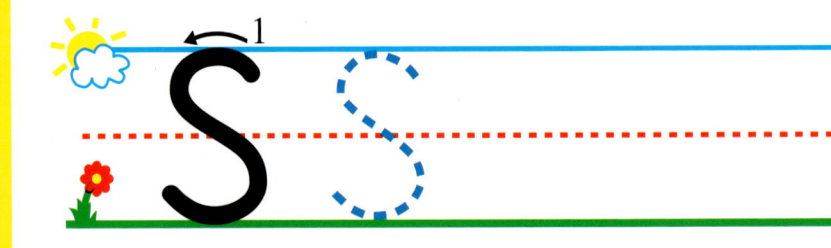

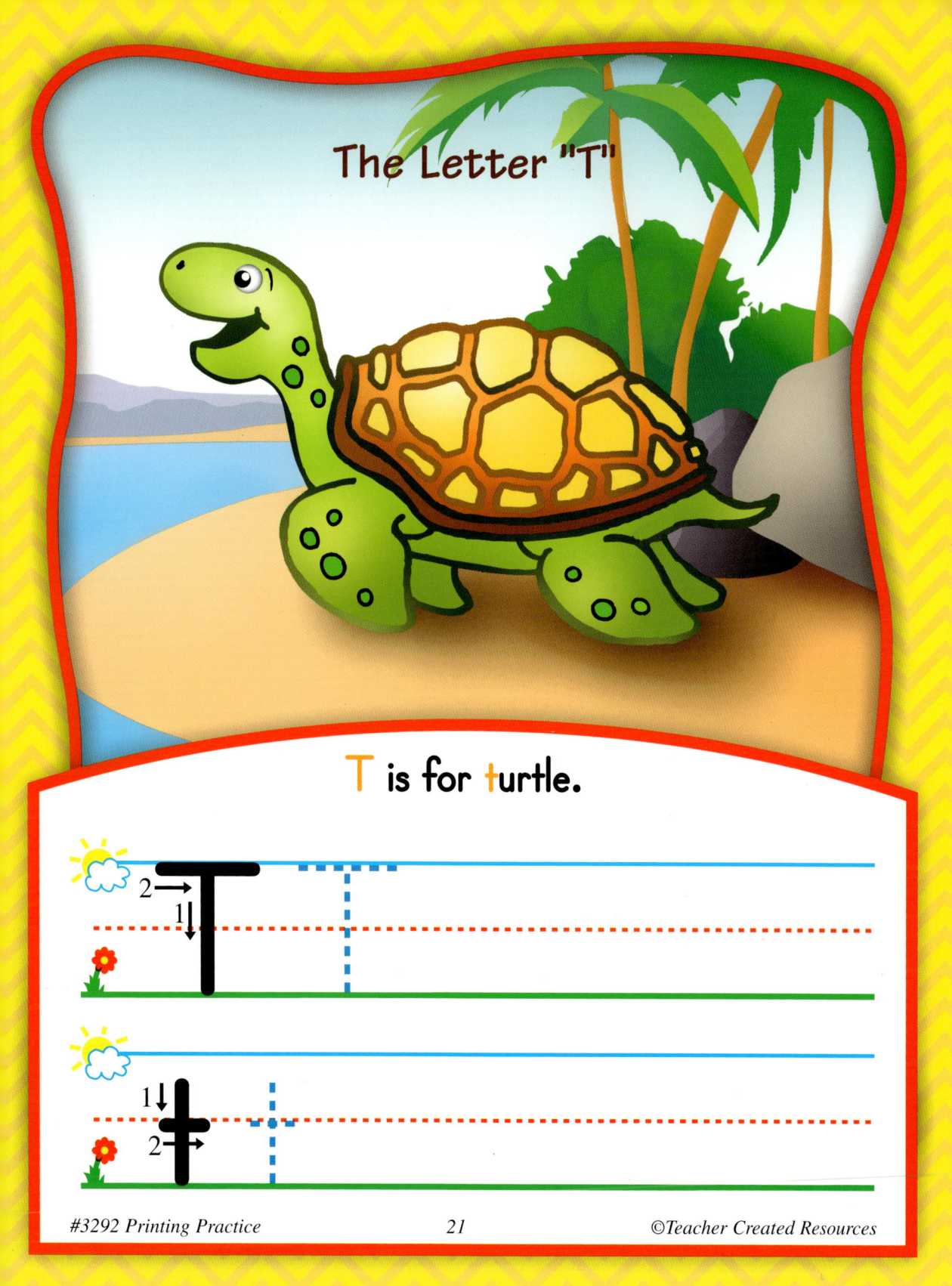

The Letter "T"

T is for turtle.

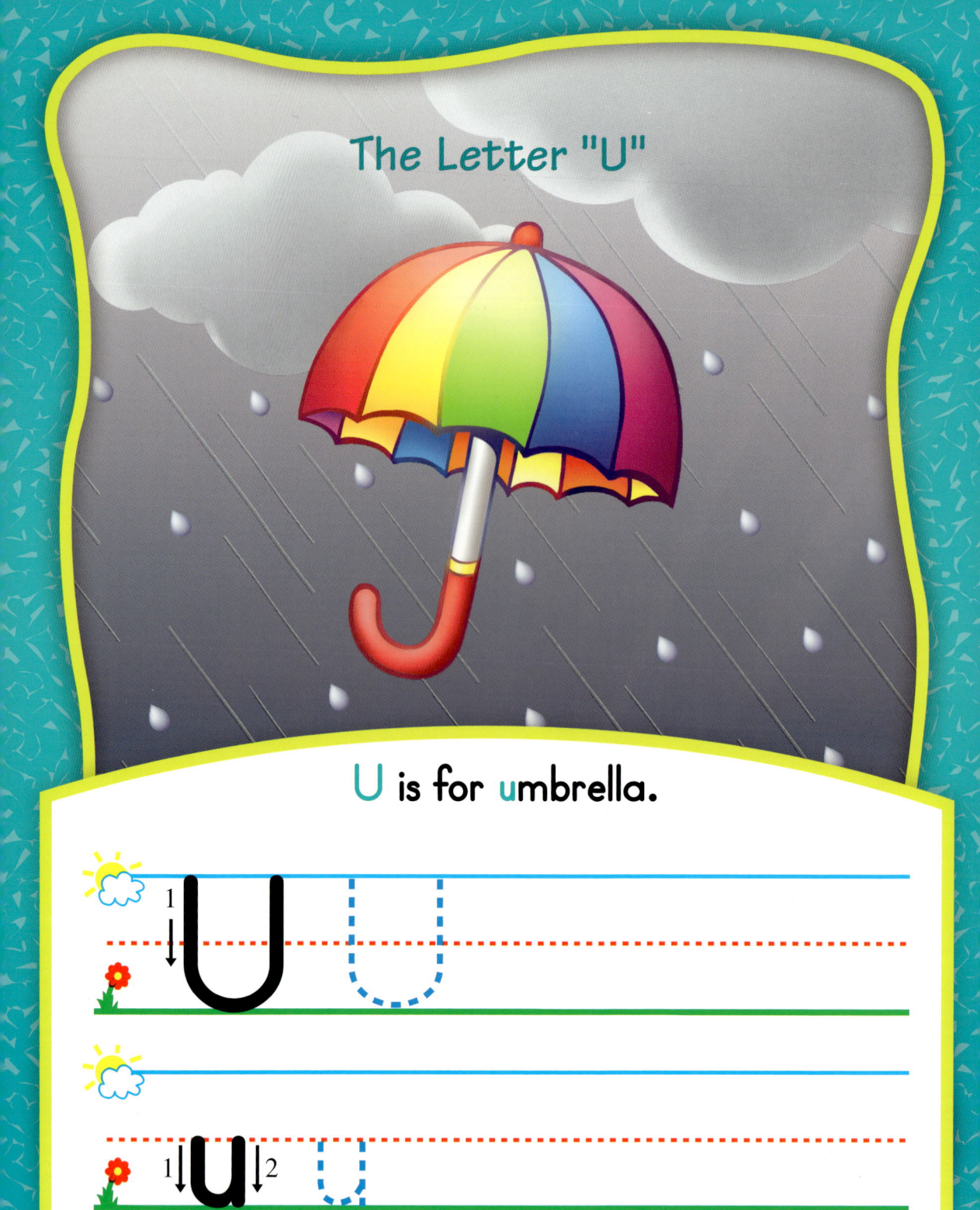

The Letter "U"

U is for umbrella.

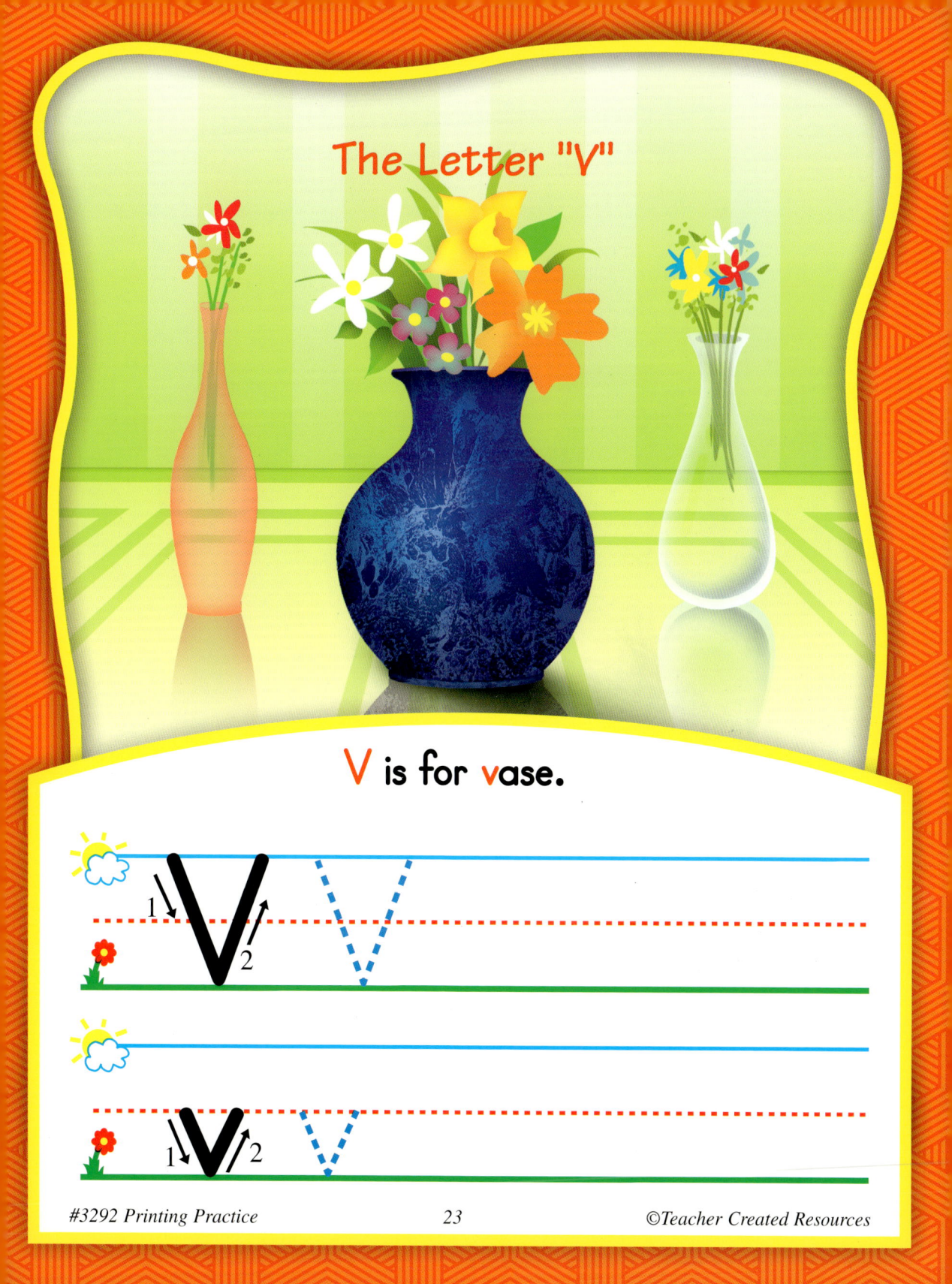

The Letter "V"

V is for vase.

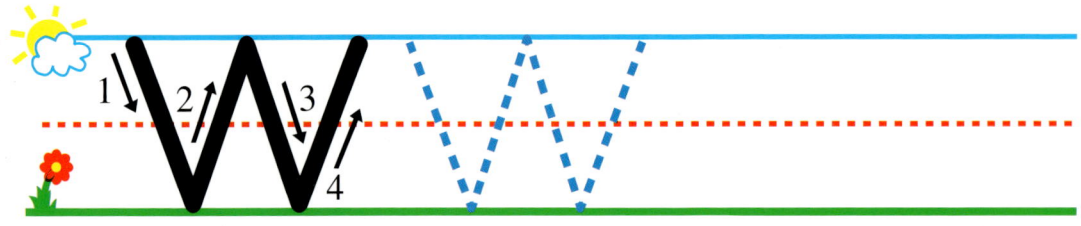

The Letter "W"

W is for wagon.

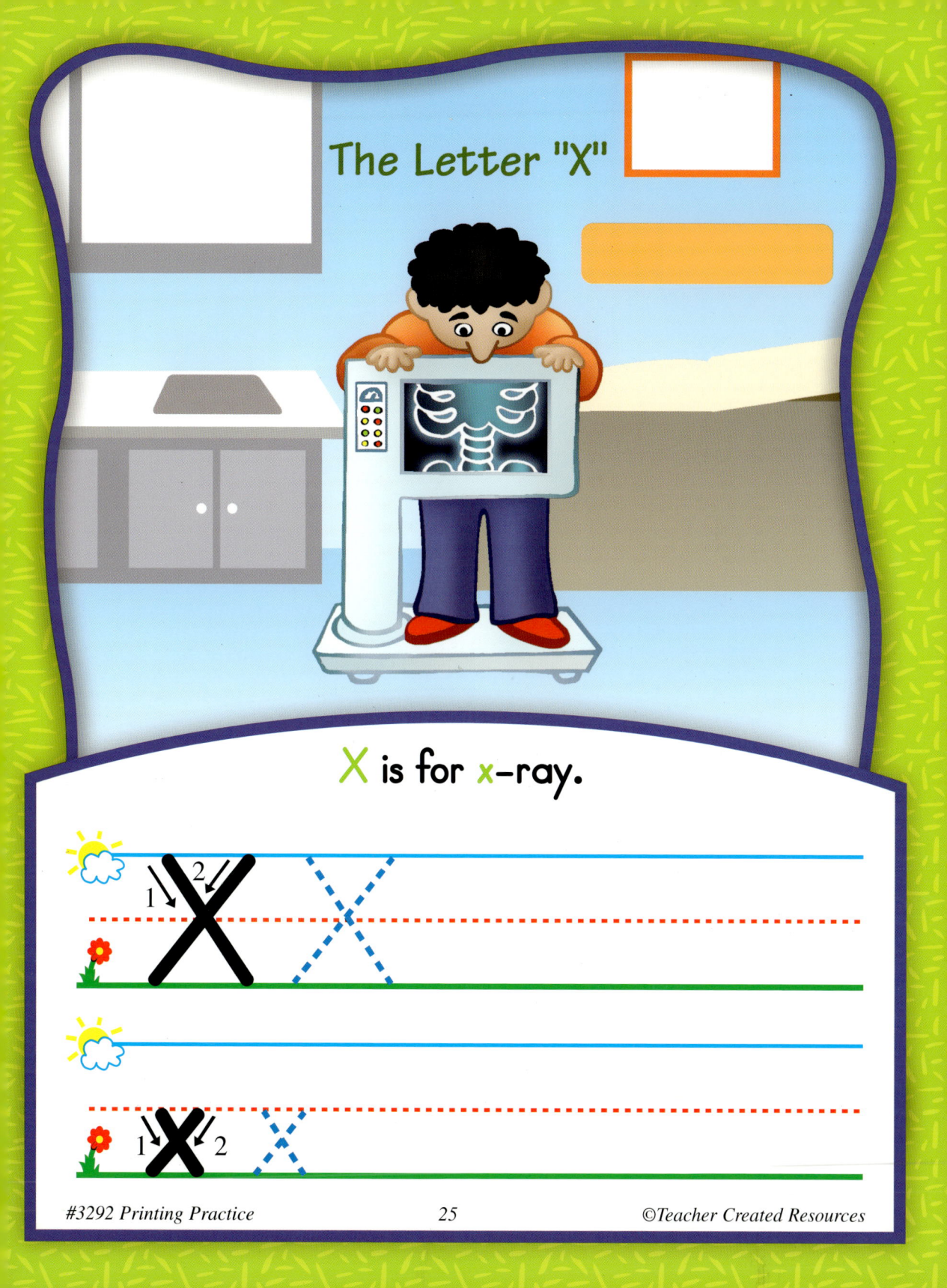

The Letter "X"

X is for x-ray.

The Letter "Y"

Y is for yoyo.

The Letter "Z"

Z is for zebra.

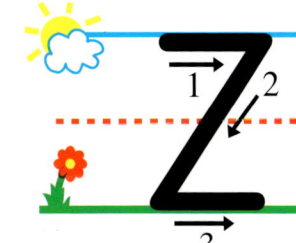

What Comes Next?

Directions: Write the next letter in each series.

A B C D ___

R S T U ___

K L M N ___

G H I J ___

C D E F ___

V W X Y ___

P Q R S ___

I J K L ___

Under the Palm (A–Z)

Directions: Connect the dots from A to Z. Start at the ★.
What did you draw?

Busy Bees (a–z)

Directions: Connect the dots from a to z. Start at the ★. What did you draw?

#3292 Printing Practice 30 ©Teacher Created Resources

Alphabet Maze

Baby Bear is hiding. Help Mama Bear follow the alphabet to find him.

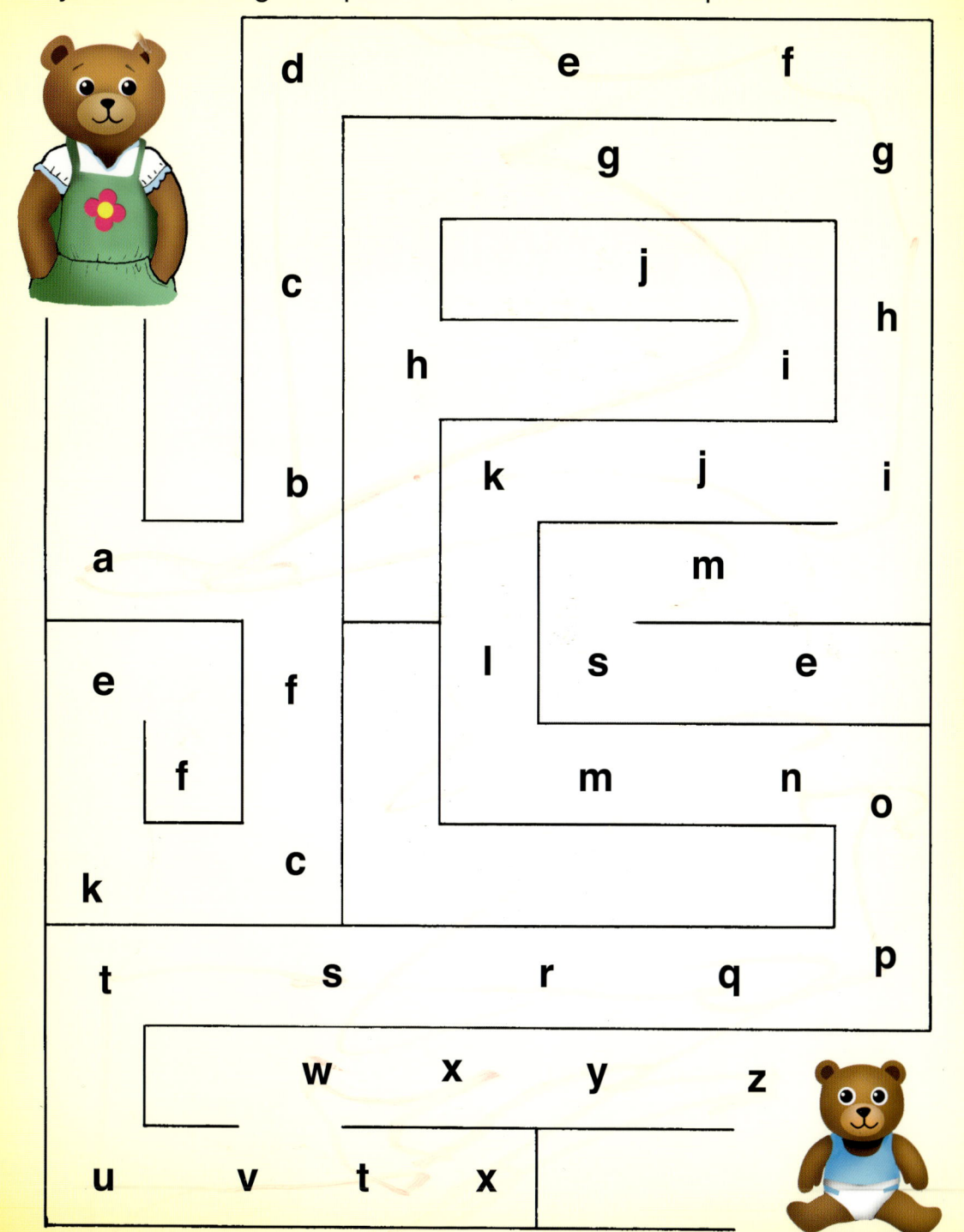

	d	e		f
		g		g
		j		h
c	h		i	
b	k	j		i
a		m		
		l s	e	
e	f			
	f	m	n	o
k	c			
t	s	r	q	p
	w	x	y	z
u	v	t	x	

#3292 Printing Practice   31   ©Teacher Created Resources

The Messy Room

Directions: Jason spilled his box of lowercase letters in his room. Help Jason find his lowercase letters. Circle the ones you find.

Practice Page

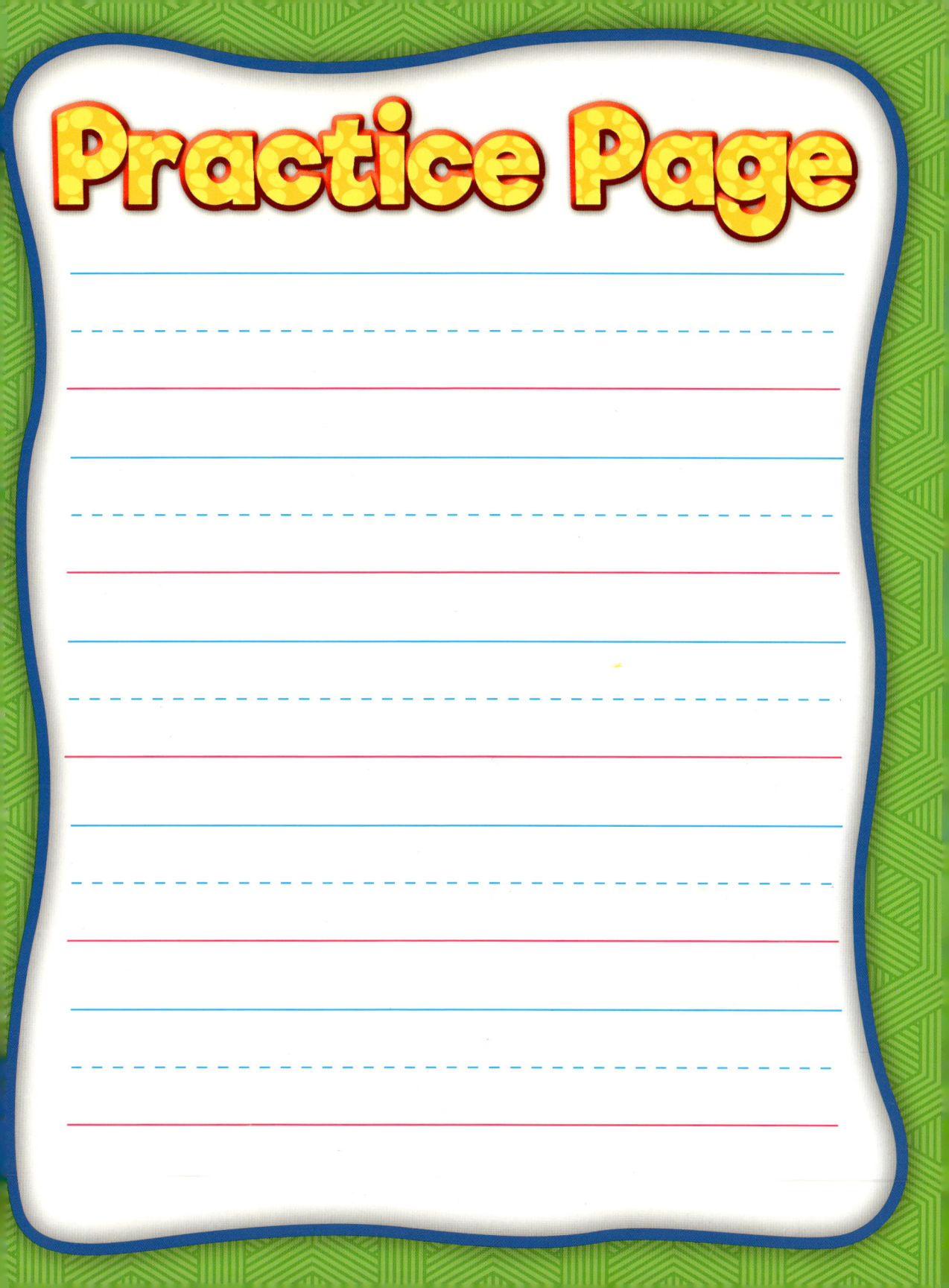

Grades K-1

WRITE-ON / WIPE-OFF

Make Learning Fun!

Write-On/Wipe-Off books are **engaging, versatile learning tools** that can be enjoyed over and over again. This book is geared toward helping children **develop and master basic skills**. Durable pages allow for easy erasing, offering endless opportunities for practice and learning fluency. The book works with all dry-erase markers—fill each page and then just **wipe away and start again**! The colorful pages and captivating activities make learning fun!

Using this book, children will…

- ✔ Develop proper printing habits
- ✔ Form uppercase and lowercase letters
- ✔ Practice using correct form, size, and spacing
- ✔ Learn how to write legibly

Related Products

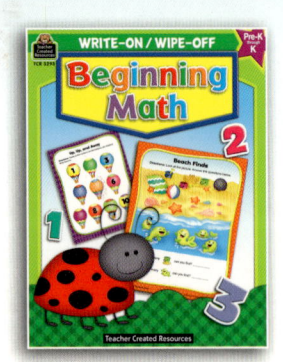

TCR 3293 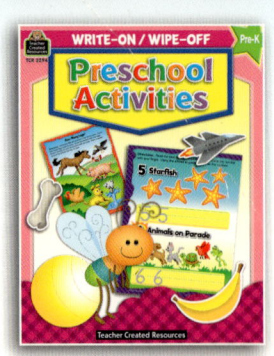   TCR 3294 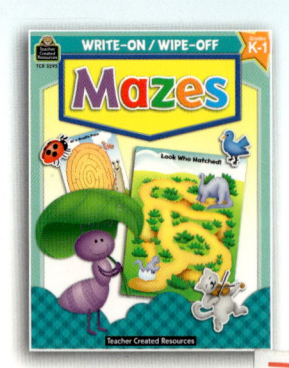   TCR 3295

USD $ 4.99

© Teacher Created Resources
Garden Grove, CA 92841

All Rights Reserved. No part of this book may be copied or reproduced in any form without written permission of the publisher.

Teacher Created Resources
www.teachercreated.com

ISBN-13: 978-1-4206-3292-7

9 781420 632927

Printed in China
PO 601036